## Turtle Light Press Haiku Chapbook Contest Winners

*The Deep End of the Sky,* Chad Lee Robinson (2015)

*The Window That Closes,* Graham High (2013)

*All That Remains,* Catherine J.S. Lee (2011)

*Sketches from the San Joaquin,* Michael McClintock (2009)

## Other Turtle Light Press Haiku Books

*Nick Virgilio: A Life in Haiku,* Nick Virgilio
(Edited by Raffael de Gruttola)

*Peace and War: A Collection of Haiku from Israel,* Rick Black

**Also by Chad Lee Robinson**

HAIKU

*Rope Marks*, Snapshot Press, 2012

*Pop Bottles*, True Vine Press, 2009

EDITED SERIES

*Gone Fishing*, a Per Diem: Daily Haiku online feature
of The Haiku Foundation, September 2014

The Deep End of the Sky

# The
# Deep
# End
# Of
# The
# Sky

## Chad Lee Robinson

*Turtle Light Press • Arlington, Va. • 2015*

*for Kimberly & for Nathan*

## I. The Tractor's Radio

at
the
deep
end
of
the
sky
prairie

meadowlark—
all you'll ever need to know
about sunrise

petals thinner
than their purple
pasque at first light




field stones
the broadness
of the farmer's back

stars at dusk:
the tractor's radio
crackles

spring rain—
speaking of the dead
in a softer voice


my grandmother's Bible—
every bookmark
an obituary

by the bait shop's old stone wall
the scattered sun
of dandelions


fishing derby
last year's winner throws back
another beer


prairie stream—
what I know about mountains
in these small stones

letting go
of the oars . . .
spring breeze

7

THE DEEP END OF THE SKYTHE DEEP END OF THE SKY

## II. Rows of Corn

night fishing
the gentle pull
of the nearest star

melon blossoms—
asking my father how it feels
to be a father

the Big Dipper—
rows of corn connect
farm to farm




my brother's gravestone . . .
under the moss a darkness
that won't come off




cemetery—
the scent of muskmelon
from the next hill

liver spots . . .
how lightly she holds
the tiger lily

what I did with my time wheatshine brightens and dims

wind in the tall grass . . .
an old blue car
almost in motion

roadside stand
cornhuskers talk
with their hands


watermelons
the weight of our grunts
breaks an axle

summer's end
a flatbed's loose chain
rattles down the road

THE DEEP END OF THE SKY

## III. Farm Lights

apple scent . . .
flecks of harvest dust
float in the wine

a steaming bowl
of new crop potatoes
September evening

evening moon—
the last bale of hay
ascends the conveyor

farm lights
halo the horizon
autumn dusk


trail of leaves
the child's plastic rake
missing teeth


resetting the bones
of the fence—
morning glory vines

pink sky
a pheasant falls through
the gunshot's echo

sunset clouds
the decoy's touch-ups
in a different hue

migrating geese—
the things we thought we needed
darken the garage

November wind
my grandmother's
unfinished sentence

mallards fly away—
darker shades of autumn
return to the river

THE DEEP END OF THE SKY

IV. Home Early


snow before dark
the field bundled
into bales


a slight shake of bells
as the harness comes off
night snow

home early—
alone in the silence
eating a bruised pear




snow deepens—
the corner drawer full
of soup labels

the sound of bath water
going down the drain
winter evening


my body thinner these days I hear more of the wind


midnight shivers
the sound of a mouse
the sound of a not-mouse

cleaning out
the dryer's lint trap—
winter solitude


hunter's retreat
the Christmas tree made from
racks of antlers

winter stars . . .
the name of my father
of my father's father

a line of rods
ready with lures
morning light

out of the depths of the mountain bluebird

ponies a pasture beyond
the last known color
in the twilight sky

a farmer sets
the curve of his cap
prairie skyline

THE DEEP END OF THE SKY

# About the Author

Chad Lee Robinson was born in 1980 in Pierre, South Dakota and grew up along the banks of the Missouri River. He continues to live there with his wife Kimberly and son Nathan, and works as the manager of his father's grocery store.

It was in 2002, Robinson's final year at South Dakota State University, that David Allan Evans, poet laureate of South Dakota, introduced him to haiku by sharing a translation of Basho's haiku about a crow on a bare branch. The attraction was immediate, and Robinson has since devoted all of his creative energy to haiku, senryu and tanka. Much of his work is about small towns and the Great Plains.

Robinson's first chapbook of haiku, *Pop Bottles*, won the 2009 True Vine Press Summer Chapbook Competition, and was published by the press that same year. His second chapbook of haiku, *Rope Marks*, was one of eight winners in the Snapshot Press e-chapbook Awards 2011, and was published in 2012.

Along with his achievements as a poet, Robinson has served the Haiku Society of America as Plains & Mountains regional coordinator (2006-2011 and again in 2014). He is also a panelist for The Haiku Foundation's Touchstone Distinguished Book Awards. Robinson also edited *Gone Fishing*, a Per Diem: Daily Haiku feature, which appeared on the website of The Haiku Foundation in September 2014.

For more information about Robinson's work, please visit his author profile at The Haiku Foundation or *Poets & Writers* magazine.

# Acknowledgements

I am grateful to the editors of the following publications and contests where most of these poems, or versions of them, first appeared:

*Acorn, bottle rockets, Frogpond, The Haiku Foundation's HaikuNow! International Haiku Contest 2010, Hermitage (Romania), The Heron's Nest, A Hundred Gourds, Mariposa, Mayfly, Modern Haiku, A New Resonance: Emerging Voices in English-Language Haiku Volume 4 (Red Moon Press, 2005), Paper Wasp (Australia), Simply Haiku, Tinywords, Walking the Same Path: Haiku Society of America Members' Anthology 2004,* and *While the Light Holds (Magnapoets, 2009).*

I'd like to thank: Penny Harter, for judging the contest and for selecting this manuscript; Rick Black, for his time and expertise, and for his many thoughtful suggestions that made this a better collection; David Allan Evans, for introducing me to haiku; all my family, for the support and inspiration. Special thanks to my wife, Kimberly, for being the first person I share new poems with, and for keeping me encouraged when the words are hard to come by.

April 2015
Pierre, South Dakota

# Colophon

The cover photo of Badlands National Park, South Dakota, is reproduced courtesy of Wing-Chi Poon, under a wikimedia creative commons license. The cover font is Charlemagne Standard; on the back cover, the font used is Constantia.

The body of this book and poems are set in Goudy Old Style. The title page panoramic of the Sand Lake National Wildlife Refuge, taken by John and Karen Hollingsworth, is reproduced courtesy of the U.S. Fish and Wildlife Service.

Photos at the end of sections one, three and four are reproduced courtesy of istockphoto.com. At the end of section two, the photo of the grain elevator in Herrick, South Dakota, is reproduced under a wikimedia creative commons license.

Grateful thanks to Penny Harter who served as judge of this chapbook competition.

CPSIA information can be obtained at www.ICGtesting.com
Printed in the USA
BVOW05s1550171215

430531BV00040B/19/P